Poems From East London

Edited By Kelly Scannell

First published in Great Britain in 2019 by:

Young Writers
Remus House
Coltsfoot Drive
Peterborough
PE2 9BF
Telephone: 01733 890066
Website: www.youngwriters.co.uk

FOREWORD

Here at Young Writers, we love to let imaginations run wild and creativity go crazy. Our aim is to encourage young people to get their creative juices flowing and put pen to paper. Each competition is tailored to the relevant age group, hopefully giving each pupil the inspiration and incentive to create their own piece of creative writing, whether it's a poem or a short story. By allowing them to see their own work in print, we know their confidence and love for the written word will grow.

For our latest competition Poetry Wonderland, we invited primary school pupils to create wild and wonderful poems on any topic they liked – the only limits were the limits of their imagination! Using poetry as their magic wand, these young poets have conjured up worlds, creatures and situations that will amaze and astound or scare and startle! Using a variety of poetic forms of their own choosing, they have allowed us to get a glimpse into their vivid imaginations. We hope you enjoy wandering through the wonders of this book as much as we have.

★ CONTENTS ★

Atika Mogal Sarfaraj (10)	73
Darshan Patel (8)	74
Amina Ali (10)	75
Samia Zahan (10)	76
Ayah Hussain (9)	77
Syed Muhammad Ali (10)	78
Ahyan Lais (8)	79
Aleeza Shah (10)	80
Suleiman Dinki (10)	81
Hamza Delawala (10)	82
Aneesah Jannat Ali (8)	83
Emir Rojah (10)	84
Taneesha Anand Patel (8)	85
Zoha Rafiq (10)	86
Mariam Hussain (10)	87
Ruman Mahomed (11)	88
Rayyan Afini (11)	89
Sofia Ahmed (10)	90
Huda Zahid (10)	91

St James' CE Junior School, Forest Gate

Jakub Czostek (9)	92
Tayyab Ahmed Hussain (10)	95
Yahyah Islam (9)	96
Maryam Ahmed (9)	97
Oniv Basu Mazumdar (8)	98
Samira Rahman (7)	100
Layali Abdul-Aziz (7)	101
Ismaeel Uzzaman (9)	102
Kayla Monica Monteiro (9)	103
Kajus Milaševičius (9)	104
Shakir Alin (9)	105
Isabelle Tunluiaru (8)	106
Aisha Saddiq (9)	107
Gabriella Mumenu Kinduku (9)	108
Hima Zubair (7)	109
Ivet Penovska (7)	110
Arta Siddique (7)	111
Rahell (9)	112
Aniyah Opoku (8)	113
Aistis Maze (7)	114
Niki Baltov (9)	115

Aleena Ahmed (9)	116
Henriqueta Djalo (9)	117
Aidan Monstaquim (8)	118
Matyas Sarosi (9)	119
Maria Galarza (9)	120
Iqlas Abukar (7)	121
Raphael Kimuli (7)	122
Sophie Chambers (9)	123
Liyana Haque (7)	124
Siyona Paliwal (9)	125
Dion Byne (7)	126
Ihsaan Uzzaman (8)	127
Rachael Oluwagbemisola Akinnifesi (7)	128
Aritz Ayomikun Akinrele (8)	129
Ethan Bennet (7)	130
Amin Mosthafa (7)	131
Zak Abdo (7)	132
Ruwaydah Alin (9)	133
Diyana Ahmed (7)	134
Renee Anselm (7)	135
Ibrahim Njie (9)	136
Khadeeja Hassan Mallu (7)	137
Alisa Emini (7)	138
Shakira Sulekhan (7)	139
Remai Peart (7)	140
Ayaan Amer (7)	141
Anayet Noor (9)	142
Marouan Ouldmakhloufi (9)	143
Farhan Omar Kazi (7)	144
Mariam Zakaria (7)	145
Abubakar Hussain (7)	146
Amirah Begum (7)	147
Destiny Boima (8)	148
Selena Saimyer (7)	149
Aleena Hoque (7)	150
Maryam Khatun (7)	151
Perla Alegra Petkeviciute (7)	152

THE POEMS

The Wonderful Magic Land

W hy don't you come and visit?
O ooh, do you want to see the mermaid fairy princess?
N ow, do you want magic cotton candy?
D o look at stuff and imagine stuff
E eek! I am so excited to go on the ride!
R un as fast as a rainbow
F eel free with everything
U p and down, why do we have to leave?
L eap and skip on a ride.

M ake a rainbow with a bow!
A wonderful trip to Magic Land
G o on the magic bus
I love trips, yay!
C atch a ride and sit down.

L eap and land on the ground
A nd skip hop, can't stop!
N early go round and round
D own and up goes the roller coaster.

Sophie Diaz (8)
Faraday School, Poplar

Gremlins

The radio shattered,
The astronauts looked worried,
"Please, your gremlin majesty," they said,
"We're very sorry."
The gremlin king said,
"Alright, you can be my guest
But your behaviour has to be
At its very best."

Before them, appeared
A huge table,
The astronauts
Did not think they were able
To eat the contents on that table.
The menu was,
Smelly socks with
Space bozz,
Mashed snot,
Beetle sausages with
Underwater bot!
Gooey sweat,
Melted nose hair,

Crusty earwax,
And the backside of a bear.

Next to this, was a table-chewing gremlin,
Who had horribly green skin,
Quickly, the table picked up a knife,
This cost the gremlin its life
For now, there was a table-chewing gremlin.

The astronauts held back their vomit,
But they could not take it
So they vomited all over the... can you call it food?

Isabelle Hemmes (9)
Faraday School, Poplar

Pugs Are Forever And Ever

P ugs are forever and ever
U nder the bed, they play all day
G o loco with pugs
S o what have you learnt?

A nd for a few more jacks
R ound up all the pugs
E nd all the bugs with pugs.

F or now, we are into the subject
O h forever, don't stop it
R ows of pugs are here
E very pug is for hugs
V icars all love pugs
E very pug is loved
R oundabouts, pugs run around.

A ll pugs have aced love
N ow all pugs are hugged but no doves
D oze is what pugs do.

E ither pugs or nothing
V iola is what pugs play
E xpect pugs to be hugged
R ugs are where pugs get snuggled.

James Harrison Oakes (9)
Faraday School, Poplar

The Wand And The Christmas Present

The day before Christmas Eve,
I didn't know what to do,
All I had was a pair of slippers
And a boring pair of shoes,
I stared up at the ceiling,
Everything was soundless,
I couldn't think of what I wanted,
For the second day was Christmas,
I finally had an idea!
It was very clever and bright,
I wrote and wrote and this is what it said,
'Could I have some fairy wings
With some splendid light?'
The next day I had climbed out of bed,
And put my letter in the box,
I hope Santa had got it,
Otherwise, I might get socks!
The next day, I opened my present,
But there wasn't only one,

A wand had come with it!
The best day had just begun.

Noora Chowdhury (7)
Faraday School, Poplar

Animal Limerick

There once was a hen-eating mouse,
Who loved to eat hens in their house.
But a hen got away,
So the mouse did not survive the day.
Now there was a hen-eating mouse!

There once was a man-eating lamb,
Who loved to eat them with some ham,
But he could not find a man,
So he hit himself with a fan.
Now there was a man-eating lamb!

There once was an elephant-eating table
Who loved to eat them when they were purple
But he ate an ant,
So when he ran, he had to pant.
Now there was an elephant-eating table!

Lucas Aung (10)
Faraday School, Poplar

Late For The Plane

P ut our things in our bag,
L eave the house and go to the
A irport, we find that there is
N o time to rest,
E ven though we want to eat.

F light is announced that it's departed, too
L ate to go to the gate
I want to fly to the plane so I
G et my wings to
H elp me fly and I was so fast, I got on but...
T urbulence started and made me fall!

Philippe Portheault (7)
Faraday School, Poplar

Mermaids That Live In Space

The mermaid was in space
There were ugly, crazy rocks
With cheese on the end
Of the huge rock
Then, it looked like it was
Going to hit me!
I felt freaked out
Horrible and terrified
I could hear ugly popping
From the huge rock
I felt the burning heat
From the huge star, the sun
Aliens came to try to eat me
But the mermaid had powers
So I am going to kill
The ugly, crazy aliens.

Inaya Jannat Miah (7)
Faraday School, Poplar

Volcano

There was once a car underwater,
He saw a volcano, *bang bang!*
This was invisible
But how could he see it then?

I still do wonder
Does it have a jumper?
No, I really need to stop
That was a really big flop
I do not have a clue.

I feel clueless
It is a good mystery indeed
A little bird told me
It is hot.

Lava, lava!
Hot, hot, hot!
Arghhhhh!

Kyle Edwards (9)
Faraday School, Poplar

The Underwater Temple

The water temple is very peaceful and graceful
It also has space
You can breathe in the water
But it feels like you are shorter.
It's really hot and nothing can stop
If you want to relax,
You should go there
There are a lot of facts
You should really come
Because you can have a lot of fun
You can eat a lot of food
So you might be in a good mood.

Laurens Hemmes (7)
Faraday School, Poplar

The Magic Football

I like to play football in the park
The game goes on till it's dark
We lost the ball in a big green bush
We went into the huge branches
With a long, hard push
I saw a shimmering golden ball
And pulled it out after a short crawl
Every time we kicked the ball, it got bigger
First to our knees
Then our bellies
It took off and flew across the trees!

Emily Wheater (7)
Faraday School, Poplar

Alive Cupcake

A cupcake lives in a land of cupcakes.
L ick me, I have rainbow icing and
I have colourful sprinkles.
V iolet cupcake with spots on it
E very bite you take is very delicious.

C innamon
U sed
P urple
C upcakes
A lways
K eep
E verything tidy in the Land of Cupcakes.

Ria Eliza Mathew (7)
Faraday School, Poplar

Foodtastic Land

I am a queen
I'm a unicorn if you didn't know
I rule Food Land
I rule animals and I rule LOLs
I live in a candy palace
Wherever you go it's edible!
It tastes so good... *mmmm!*
Animals don't eat each other
Because everything is edible!
Cupcakes, pizza, cookies, it all tastes so good.
I love my life, so does everybody else.

Zahra Estella Eriksson Alom (7)
Faraday School, Poplar

The Shark Ate My Ears!

I fell into a shark's den and it swallowed my ears!
The shark said, "Bubble, bubble,"
And I fell into tears
I said, "Mr Shark, why are my ears lollipops?"
And the shark said, "Bubble, bubble."
I screamed with rage
I thought it was a dream
But I woke up in the shark's tummy.

Felicity Reed (7)
Faraday School, Poplar

My Vampire Poodle

My vampire poodle,
Why is he evil?
I don't know.
When he wants to, he can be
As sweet as a cock-a-doodle
But when he wants to
In the dead of night
He'll creep and crawl
And chew your toes
And he's got a haul
Of humans bones!

Coco Zatorski (9)
Faraday School, Poplar

Silly Space Is My Place

I live in a wacky space world,
It is very strange indeed,
There are jelly dinosaurs and rainbow puke,
You may come if you please.

In this place, unexpected things
Are all around,
Burgers and elephants with mullets,
Far above the ground.

Tortoise surfing,
Significantly crazy,
Singing purple stars,
Soft as a daisy.

Stars singing heavy metal jingle bells,
Everywhere I go,
My cockerel is puking rainbows,
It's so crazy - oh!

The jelly dinosaur has rocket skateboards,
And purple mushroom lasers,

Bang bang bang!
My cockerel's claws are as sharp as razors!

I live in a wacky space world,
It is very strange indeed,
There are jelly dinosaurs and rainbow puke,
You may come if you please.

There are purple stars,
Singing heavy metal jingle bells,
Strange brown mushrooms,
Scented with bluebell smells.

You say we cannot breathe in space,
'Cause there is no air
But here, oxygen is mint-scented
Plus there is magic everywhere!

Monster clouds in the sky
Whilst there are devouring pot-pie,
And being stalked by a fly,
On the top of a massive eye!

Mia Berou (9)
Normanhurst School, North Chingford

Best Burger!

Below the hole,
Under the snow,
There's a land
It's not a beach, there's no sand,
It's a wonderland!
There's a burger band
It's a mouse inside a burger house
In the woods, there isn't a woodlouse
It's amazing
The stars are gazing,
It doesn't matter where you walk,
You can just talk
Next to the house, there is a ketchup bank
A burger sank whilst playing a plank,
The burger mountain is bigger than Mount Everest.

Let's not go to Mount Everest, it needs a rest
A burger has a plan
It's going to put a pie in a pram,
Oh, it's great to be here
We're going to drink some beer
Well, that's not all

I've got a burger stall
Burgers are cool
They don't go to school
And that's all
Let's get a burger ball.

Konrad Nosek (9)
Normanhurst School, North Chingford

How I Lost My Best Friend

One day, I went to the ocean,
And I brought two things with me,
Lotion to put on by the ocean,
And my pet chihuahua named Pippy.

She barked and yapped
As loud as an elephant
It drove me crazy!

When we got there,
I opened the door and
She ran into the sand
Into the ocean and back on land.

I put on some lotion
And ran into the ocean
And got wet.

We went into the ocean again
And got all soaking wet
Then the biggest ever wave came
That I have ever seen.

You'll never believe it,
But it is true,
The wave took Pippy Sue!

I cried and cried
And I blame myself,
I will always remember Pippy.

I returned to the beach
And I realised Pippy is a wave now
I know where to go if I feel lonely.

Mattea Tosh (8)
Normanhurst School, North Chingford

The Exploding Soda

W hen I was at school, I suddenly spotted an unusual thing, it was an

O dd-looking thing which looked like it was a very peculiar pickle with a

N odding nose, which looked like they were doing a high-five, after that they

D ozed off to sleep, they all fell to the floor and then rose. Next, they

E nded upside down; after a minute or so, they sneezed and they all

R andomly disappeared like magic. When I sat down, I realised that they had

L anded on top of the soda machine, and were now making it go bonkers.

A fter a few moments, the soda machine suddenly exploded, and a

N ew kind of flavour popped into my mouth. It was unusual - how

D o I describe it? It was obviously broccoli-flavoured soda!

Imogen Whitfield (8)
Normanhurst School, North Chingford

Night Night

I was at the circus, watching a clown,
To be honest, I don't know why he had a frown.
He could be joking, he could be not,
Can I say he looked really cross?

He had half a cyborg face
And half a clown face,
He had really nice shoes,
But a really bad lace.

He was called Night Night and he was really scary,
He really was the opposite of a fairy,
I am really not trying to be rude,
Honest, I am just telling the truth.

At the end of the show,
He called me to the stage,
I actually thought he was about to rage.
He spoke and said, "Make an impression of me."

He said his actual name was Tim,
So here it went,
I just played with the tent.

Kelaiah Ifeanyi Elba (9)
Normanhurst School, North Chingford

Expecto Patronum!

E xpecto Patronum against Dementors
X enophilius Lovegood, a good mentor
P everell brothers and the Hallows
E xpecting Harry to die at Godric's Hollow
C harlie Weasley's with dragons
T he Dark Lord will steal it
O n the way with Floo powder.

P otter asking, "Why so many flowers?"
A lbus Potter, the cursed child
T he son of a lawmaker trialled
R on, a friend of The Boy Who Lived
O f course, Hermione complained of Harry's quiff
N one of the Horcruxes left unscathed
U nicorns, the Dark Lord slayed
M ighty Slytherin, Ravenclaw, Hufflepuff and Gryffindor!

Alfie Hunt (10)
Normanhurst School, North Chingford

Underwater Restaurant

W e were soaking wet and soggy

O n the day that we went to the restaurant, it made me think of fish

N ear a sabre-toothed fish by the window of the restaurant

D own by the sea, there was a restaurant and outside the restaurant, in the open, there was a shark

E verything in the restaurant was all wet and covered in water

R ed and blue little fish swimming past the window, it was lovely

L adies in the restaurant don't wear dresses, it's just jeans and shorts

A nd there is an octopus and a jellyfish, starfish

N ever stop eating in the underwater restaurant

D own by the sea, near the restaurant, there was a shark.

Bella Ward (7)

Normanhurst School, North Chingford

Cotton Candy Clouds

C otton candy clouds are free

O n the winds

T hey're not tidy and

T here are more than two

O ver the Earth, very fluffy and pink

N obody likes the cotton candy clouds like I do.

C otton candy clouds are wonderland themed

A lso, a wonderful thing

N ever underestimate the power of clouds, they

D o not speak or dance but they let

Y our imagination run wild.

C otton candy clouds are lovely and

L ots of fun

O ver your head and

U nder the stars

D one with the normal clouds and yes with the new

S ometimes, it's just about you.

Amber Cook (9)

Normanhurst School, North Chingford

Cat

There I was, walking down the road
And *poof!* I became a bird
Then a rat
Then a cat.

There I was, walking down the road as a cat
I stepped on the mat and miaowed like a cat
Then my mum came out and said,
"Oh, a cat, it looks like a rat."
She shut the door in my face.

I ran away like I was in a race
Then I found another cat
We became friends and chased rats
When we caught one
I ate it as fast as the speed of light.

"Ewww, it tastes like fur!"
Poof! I turned into a bird
Then a lion
Then a cat
Then a rat
And now a mat?

Margarida Lopes Da Silveira (11)
Normanhurst School, North Chingford

Roller Ants

Trousers stay on, go away pants,
I'm on a roller coaster with ants,
Not just any coaster,
I won't be a boaster,
But an anteater roller coaster.

I am in an upside down world
With my best buddy, Arnold,
There's a loop-de-loop,
And a bit of gloop,
Super speed,
A few little weeds,
Yes!

Twisting around the inner-state,
Cleaning up butter and rubber snakes,
It's making me haul,
Twisting around the mall
Oh yeah!

Sitting on a chair,
With my whipping hair,
A bit bare,

My teacher, Miss Clair,
Moving some gum,
Yummy in my tum,
Yum yum yum!
That is done!

Douglas Morris (9)
Normanhurst School, North Chingford

The Talking Flower

I'm in my room
I heard a *boom!*
I screamed out loud
"What's all this about?"

I looked outside
There I saw
A talking flower
"Hello!" it said.

I was too surprised to say anything
So I turned away and took
One step - it whispered out,
"I'm your friend."
And asked,
"Did you speak more?"
I was so gobsmacked
I blinked and winked
It was still
I threw a shoe
It said nothing

So I went
Down the stairs
And had a shake
Now I'm awake
Maybe I'll also have
A midnight chocolate cake!

Shaunella Griffith (10)
Normanhurst School, North Chingford

The Aliens

W onderful, blue, shiny pupils that wander around here

O val ship, up on top of the sky and they so often come down

N ear, above the whole solar system

D own the curvy hill, they live and their favourite is

E ating alien berries from a nice delicious berry tree

R acing past the clouds, the aliens race people

L ove to cheer on, the streets are full of people that are terrified of

A liens when they walk past the town

N ear the hill, people are getting used to the aliens when they go there

D warves always get terrified when the aliens walk past.

Matteo Payne (8)

Normanhurst School, North Chingford

Life Upside Down

It's not easy living upside down
Or you'd be in such a crowd
You might think it is easy
But it really is a doozy
If you dropped something,
You would think it's fallen on the ground.
But it's really drowned
Upside down, scientists say
There really is no way.
So we're stuck like this
And the luck is yours
So don't worry, you should be sorry
You're in a strong lorry
We are jealous that your Earth's gorgeous
So don't have a cow and come right now
Maybe you should feel our pain
Down in a drain.

Sevan Polat Ulus (9)
Normanhurst School, North Chingford

My Amazing Dogs

There went Freeway the Dog,
Then Ralph,
Zooming past on their roller skates
Being best mates.

They were amazing
The best thing I saw
I really hoped
They would do some more.

Suddenly, they stopped
I wondered why
Then I saw it
In the sky.

It was massive
A giant bone
Floating down,
Landing on a stone.

The dogs went mad,
It was bacon flavour

The tastiest bone
They've ever had.

They took the bone
And zoomed back home
And shared it out
Without a shout.

Sophie Lang (10)
Normanhurst School, North Chingford

Crazyland

W hen I was riding a red candy, I was so happy

O bay is the blue super zing with a huge army

N eptune is where all of the lovely toys get to live

D inosaurs are red but they go to Mars, not Neptune

E verything in Earth is beautiful except for the red candy

R ed is Wonderland's favourite colour

L ight is only on Mars and sometimes on Earth,

A nd no one in Wonderland likes dinosaurs

"N ever ever give up if you don't feel good," said Obay

D inosaurs have a funny history.

Zain Shah (7)

Normanhurst School, North Chingford

The Terrible Desert

I was in the hottest desert
You can clearly see
You don't want to be there
It is the worst place to me.
I was as bored as hell
As I heard everybody yell
Then comes an icy lightning bolt rapidly
We all stayed close together weirdly
I heard screaming and shouting
As I kept crouching
Kaboom went the desert
It was freezing cold
As someone just rolled
It was as loud as a bell
We were all so frightened
As I said it is hell
The desert was gone forever
And I was as happy as ever!

Alicia Makanjuola (9)
Normanhurst School, North Chingford

The Pirate Ship

W hen I was walking, I found a treasure chest,

O h, the glamorous treasure chest had fritter coins,

N ext, freedom jewellery

D own I went, to see my glamorous pirate ship

E nd of the ship had a pirate that was an old pirate

R an to the back of the narrow, sturdy ship, next to the old room

L and was a very unhappy place with an exploding cannon

A lso, someone from another ship found us

N ext, we had a furious pirate battle

D own to get a photo with my whole group.

Tiago Makanjuola (7)

Normanhurst School, North Chingford

Wonderland's Come To Life

W onderland in the distance,

O n the street was green and leafy,

N o one seemed to mind

D own by the leafy forest, cold and dark, it was very scary!

"E eeek!" I said as a tree walked past

"R eally!" I said to myself. "I just got scared by a tree!"

L iving plants all over the place,

A Venus Flytrap ate my meal,

N othing like I have ever seen before

D idn't know what I could have done but what a day, I have had.

Orson Wilkin (7)
Normanhurst School, North Chingford

The Space Race

I'm flying into space,
And it's a race,
I hope I win,
I'll do anything to get that golden pin.

But this isn't a three-legged or egg and spoon,
The finishing line is on the moon,
I hope I see the sun,
It will be a whole lot of fun.

I may sleep along the way,
In my ship, I'll lay,
"What's that?" I say six hours later,
Did I just see a roller skater?

"Yes, we're nearly there!"
My next stop is the golden pin to wear.

Atilla Ozgur Baristiran (10)
Normanhurst School, North Chingford

Rainbows

Raining colours in the air
Very nice to glare
It's a shiny new record
It's an angel in harmony
And it sounds like an A-chord.
On the other side,
There's some money
And next to it, there's some honey.
Then, there is a leprechaun
All of a sudden, a new rainbow is born
With the money, I can get a Lambo
So I call my friend, Rambo
This is my rainbow
I call it Dodo
I don't know why.
A few minutes later, I had to say bye-bye
I cried, my soul had died.

Emmanuel Jordan Oloke (11)
Normanhurst School, North Chingford

The Monster Who Came To Tea

He sat down
And took a seat,
He was all scruffy
Not at all neat.

Ice cream, doughnuts,
Cookies, cakes,
Soda, chips and
Chocolate shakes
That's all he ate!

Now the fridge is clear
I want this monster to disappear
Because he has given me an awful fear!

Now here's some good advice:
Don't let a monster come to tea
Even if he looks nice.

And here's another tip:
When he starts to lick his lips
Remember to run and scream!

Ella Mycroft (10)
Normanhurst School, North Chingford

Wonderland

Objects you thought so innocent
Can turn your mind down side up,
In Wonderland!

Candy cats battle toothpaste tubes, viciously,
Toothbrushes versus chocolate chicks
Mouthwash guarding with gobstoppers.

Dirty, smelly gym socks
Fight washing machines
Hungry vacuums hunt dusty sofas,
Dripping mops assault slimed tiles.

Defenceless dragons clash with bold knights
Brainless cyclops wrestle with intelligent heroes
Fire demons brawl with water demons.

Finley David Alpha Bird (10)
Normanhurst School, North Chingford

The Dragon Who Lives In Wonderland

W hen I ride my blue, fierce dragons, I get scarred
O n my chest and it hurts
N ot the best thing to happen in your life
D on't ever get a big blue dragon!
E ven if you're old enough.
R ed, green, yellow and orange aren't so bad!
L ong-necked and short-necked are fierce
A nd blue dragons are the fiercest of them all!
N ever look a blue dragon in the eye,
D on't touch its blue, shiny scales.

Max Young (7)
Normanhurst School, North Chingford

Maclarens

M agnificent beauty
A nd power
C an make you glare
L ike a long, long stare
A s an animal would to a person
R esponding like a beast
E ast to west, sleep and rest!
N ever end, never stop, never ever drop
S ee everything.

A nd feel it too
R ecreate your destiny
E nhance your IQ.

C ome and see
O ur cool and
O ur secret
L egacy.

Chioke Tafari Meade (11)

Normanhurst School, North Chingford

Candyland

W alking on a bouncy street, waiting for a sweet bus

O n the tasty day, it came

N ice and delicious, I was going to Candyland

D own by the road of Candyland, there was a tasty lollipop

E verybody was getting blocked by it

R ight, I can imagine that a dragon can help

L isten and you can hear Candyland!

A big dragon lets us into Candyland

N ow, I'm leaving Candyland, it was great

D one, I fall asleep!

Leo Karamanlis (7)

Normanhurst School, North Chingford

Candyland

W alking along the sticky, hard path

O n a charming sunny day

N ot much trouble in Candyland

D oing candy games all day

E verybody was having a great time

R ed, blue and purple are the town's favourite coloured sweets

L iquorice ropes are hanging from the ceiling in the gym

A nts are having a great time playing ants and ladders

N othing horrible is happening in Candyland

D oing everything right.

Ilayda Jelal (7)

Normanhurst School, North Chingford

About The Lion

W hen I went to the spooky park,

O n this day, I saw a strange lion who was as green as grass

N ever seen this lion in my life

D on't run, in case it eats you

E veryone stood still because the lion got out of its cage

R oaring loudly to scare people

L ondon has gone crazy

A s the lion broke out of its cage

N ow the lion is dancing happily

D on't worry, the lion is a herbivore.

Zachary Shakeel (8)
Normanhurst School, North Chingford

Wonderful Wonderland

W hen I went home

O n my magic bike

N o chickens were on the floor, then suddenly...

D runk chickens rained down

"E vacuate!" I exclaimed fearfully, but then it...

R ained fish, not ordinary fish, magic fish!

"L ovely, I needed this!" I shouted, then...

A drunk chicken walked to me

N ow, I got a pet and his name is...

D onald the Chicken and he is my friend.

Dylan Thomas Evans (9)
Normanhurst School, North Chingford

Wonderland Under Attack

W hen you enter the nice candy city,
O ne of the buildings is sour,
N o one knows about Captain Candy Strike,
D ark villains don't stand a chance!
E veryone's beloved, he has a green belt,
R oyalty isn't him, he really is Peter Sweeter.
L ovely yummy people roam the streets
A nd light flows within everybody
N obody likes the terrifying
D ark pumpkin.

William Ingles (7)
Normanhurst School, North Chingford

Taco Tuesday

W here, where is my underwear?

O n the loose, here and there

N ow everybody has disturbing hair

D ad is dancing with the polar bears

E ven my old pants are growing hair

R eally, really, my underwear is there

L ots of tacos raining everywhere

A nd the tacos are jumping in the air

N ever have I seen this before

D reaming to eat the delicious tacos off the floor.

Tiago Almeida Moutou (8)

Normanhurst School, North Chingford

Bad Day

W hen I went home,

O pened the door

N othing was there except a magic banana

D ownstairs was a vacuum cleaner which never stopped cleaning

E xcellent plants growing in a garden

R eally shiny butterflies coming through the window

L eaking taps flooding everywhere

A ll around me water is rising

N ow, I am swimming

D oor opens, the water starts rushing out.

Callan Umunna (8)

Normanhurst School, North Chingford

Wonderland

W hen I was going for a walk,

O n the way, I saw a flying cat

N ear the cat was a rusty, round house

D ogs were jumping up and down

E veryone was sprinting to the end of the world

R oosters were making pizza

L ambs were wearing roller skates

A eroplanes were flying upside down

N ow I saw the pilot hanging from his chair

D ucks were wearing suits.

Saif Khan (8)

Normanhurst School, North Chingford

Not A Normal Day

W hen I went to Wonderland, I saw women that have pig noses

O ctopuses singing ever so loudly

N annies dancing everywhere

D octors dancing away in the night

E legant spiders running around

R ats wearing funny glasses

L aughing horses galloping

A nd slime that's raining from the sky

N o one knows what is going on

D efinitely not a normal day.

Olivia Maw (8)

Normanhurst School, North Chingford

Race In Space

I'm having a race,
All the way in space,
Whizzing past stars and Mars,
Scaly aliens and satellites,
"I hope to win!"

Passing black holes
And my favourite team is scoring goals
"I'm first!"
But the other rocket
Is right behind me
"On full power!"

"Oh yes! I won,
I won the golden
Solar system!"

Kian Khilosia (11)
Normanhurst School, North Chingford

Cupcakes

On a Monday morning,
I went to the park, shall I say,
And in there was a cupcake,
It was also rather big
So I went on it and bounced a little
And I flew like a bird
I ended up on a cloud, yes I did!

Then I saw a flying unicorn
It was fluffy, soft
And snow white
When I thought nothing could be better,
There was a bunny on the unicorn,
Yes indeed!

Prottusha Saha (9)
Normanhurst School, North Chingford

Dragons

Dragons,
Wonderful creatures
With fiery breath
And pointy teeth.

Wings of speed
And scales they need
They can beat you in a race
As they take the lead.

They live up high
In the mountain tops
If you see one
You're in luck.

But just so you know
You better run
For, if they see you
Their toasty breath will hit you.

Hudson Tosh (10)
Normanhurst School, North Chingford

The Real Story Of Breakfast

B reakfast is the best, just imagine

R iding some cornflakes,

E ven though it is raining sugar

A nd using a Rice Krispie to row your boat,

K onrad was the captain of the boat,

"F ull steam ahead!" he said

A nd he fell into the milk bowl

S till cheerful

"T errible captain!" we said.

Charlie Thistethwaite (9)
Normanhurst School, North Chingford

You Better Believe It

You better believe it,
Because it's definitely true
A lie is a lie,
And the truth is the truth
You better believe it,
It is true, ghosts are real,
They're not a lie, they are real,
"Go in, go in, I dare you!"
Hear the ghosts say, "Oooooh!"
He goes in without fear
He sees a ghost
Told you so, ghosts are real!

Poppy Brock (10)
Normanhurst School, North Chingford

Wonderland

W omen carrying big pigs

O ctopuses wearing silly wigs

N o horrible hogs

D riving, entertaining dogs

E lephants learning subtraction

R abbits learning addition

L eaves learning lots of English

A nd chickens acting quite sillyish

N oses as big as blue balloons

D olls dodging macaroons.

Matias Chechile (8)

Normanhurst School, North Chingford

The Chocolate Car

W ho is driving that car?
O n a summer's roasting day
N obody had ever seen that kind of car,
D elicious chocolate car
E veryone is amazed
R ed, white and black
L ittle too big, yummy chocolate car
A nd we ate the car
N othing that we can do,
"D id we have fun?" I asked.

Caleb Tosh (7)
Normanhurst School, North Chingford

Cookie Tree

W alking on the fluffy garden,

O n a nice, beautiful day

N ear the nice park

D own by the tasty cookie tree

E verything is good as a puppy

R ed, brown and black

L ovely cookies rolling down the hill

A nd nice fluffy clouds

N ever-ending fun

D own by the cookie tree.

Sienna Patel (7)

Normanhurst School, North Chingford

All About The Cheese

I went to the library, I saw some cheese
I was about to take a bite
But it just said, "Please."

The cheese grew arms and legs and it said,
"I can change back and forth
And even to an egg."

I said, "What a funny egg
Or whatever you are.
But I must be going so...
Ta-ta!"

Isabelle Young (10)
Normanhurst School, North Chingford

The Weird House

W omen wearing wigs,

O ranges turning into pigs,

N ever seen it before

D oes anyone know about this,

E verything floating

R aining inside,

L and pigs from the sky,

A nd how did this happen?

N o way

D id I just dream?

Roni Amet Kabayel (8)

Normanhurst School, North Chingford

The Fish Couldn't Climb Trees

Simon the Fish splished and splashed,
And dashed about the river weeds,
He whizzed and whooshed
And twisted through the water
Round the sticks and reeds.
He swam at speed, this way and that,
Jumped from the water with a spin,
He felt the air against his scales,
The grinned a grin and plopped back in.
"Hey fish, hey fish," he heard as he was swimming,
He saw an octopus, he saw it was swimming.
Simon just ignored him and he went
Then a rabbit popped up and he said,
"You can't climb trees." Then he said,
"I will do it," but soon after,
He went out of the water
And he didn't know that he couldn't breathe.
Then he was surprised that he couldn't breathe,
After he noticed he couldn't climb the tree,

Soon, he couldn't be happy and free.
After, the rabbit picked him up and
Put him back in the water and was banned!

Krish Patel (9)

Shaftesbury Primary School, Forest Gate

Alice Reads The Map

I once found a very weird map
While I was sitting on a mat
It said to find a rabbit hole
While I was walking,
I saw a trail of poles leading to the hole!
I went inside and saw a flying chair
But then... something fell on my hair
Then I said, "That's not fair."
Suddenly, I found a green rabbit
I followed it in a habit!
Then, when I came out of the hole...
I was in a different world
I was surprised because I found butterfly bread!
It was in my head
When I carried on, I saw a caterpillar smoking
And he was poking his own eyes
Then it was time for me to go to my mum...
But then I wanted gum.

Yusuf Isa Ahmad (8)
Shaftesbury Primary School, Forest Gate

Hear Books Talking

As I hear books talking,
I just don't know what's going on.
The day was almost gone.
As I checked every section,
They all just had lots of letters
I found one book
That I thought was very precious
I picked number two of the book
And you would not believe what I found
The whole shelf comes out
I discovered something strange
But I'm not quite sure
What it is meant to be.
I carried on walking
But I couldn't quite see
Because it was so dark.
I found a box and it had some rocks
All of a sudden, the door shut.

Maryam Patel (10)
Shaftesbury Primary School, Forest Gate

The Silly Genie

A genie flew above the cloudy sky
But silly him, he forgot to do his tie
He met an ugly dragon on his way
Why did he have to ruin the beautiful day?

The genie flew to the summer school fair
Where he fell and lost all of his hair
He felt ugly so he bought a new wig
Sadly, he wasted his money because it was too big.

He wanted an owner to rule him all day
When he found out someone wanted to buy him,
He thought, *yay!*
The genie went back into his lamp,
While the owner went into the jungle to camp.

Musa Khan (11)
Shaftesbury Primary School, Forest Gate

I Fell Down A Rabbit Hole

I fell down a rabbit hole,
A hole probably dug by a mole,
When I fell down, I saw a beautiful crown,
But it turned all brown,
There were so many mushrooms,
It was so dirty, I needed a broom,
There was a BTS army,
I felt like eating Barny.

There were so many birds,
All in a herd
Elephants that were really grey
Are we in May?
There were so many fruits
Did they put me on mute?

There were buckets of paint,
Owned by a saint,
There were beautiful flowers,
With a lot of cool powers.

Atika Mogal Sarfaraj (10)
Shaftesbury Primary School, Forest Gate

Different

I am differently able, maybe you are too
I feel overwhelmed with different sounds,
You might enjoy the entire movie
But I enjoy the closing credits more
More than songs from the movie,
I enjoy the background score.
Kids of my age enjoy
Playing with electronic gadgets
Or sports toys, but not me
I like toys which enhance my motor skills
You might find washing machines monotonous
Or humdrum, but not me
Jumping on trampolines is my passion
Jumping up high on it,
Gives me a strong feeling of freedom.

Darshan Patel (8)
Shaftesbury Primary School, Forest Gate

The Library Of Magical Books

There was a library of magical books
Sitting on the shelf, giving weird looks
As soon as the library closed down,
All the books went and looked around.

As soon as a minute went past
They were flying around so fast
One said, "Hi!" to his friend
And partied all night, it never ends.

Then a mermaid came and joined them
She had sparkly glitter and a shiny gem
Then came a time to say goodbye
Tomorrow, again, they will say hi.

Amina Ali (10)
Shaftesbury Primary School, Forest Gate

Imagination

Using your own imagination,
Can you make a donation
Will you think about our imagination?

Station is a nation
If you use your own imagination
So join us along with the poetry wonderland
Where it is best for you
And where you can rest.

Run wild with us
Then we will make you smile
The whole day is fun
You will be happy for the rest of your life.

This is a planet where
You have peace and you will see the sea.

Samia Zahan (10)
Shaftesbury Primary School, Forest Gate

If I Were At Unicorn Land

I fell down a rabbit hole,
Into a magic land,
Flying beds in the air,
Hitting me like they just don't care.

As soon as I touch a horn,
I feel magic fizzing around me,
Stepping on chocolate poop,
While jumping through a hoop.

As time passes quickly, I'm in a sweet pool,
Munching quickly on the lollipop body
And I said, "I'll come every day!"
With a jump, loop and a hiss, I went with Clay!

Ayah Hussain (9)
Shaftesbury Primary School, Forest Gate

Robo World

Riding on a lightning bolt,
With my robot drinking salt
Frying cheesy moon rocks,
While my robot is chasing a fox.

Learning to speak the alien race,
While my robot eats toxic waste,
In the garage, fixing a mech
With my robot, watching Shrek.

Surfing an erupting volcano's lava,
With my robot in a palaver
Going to the vet to fix a shark's tooth
While my robot is messing around
In the photo booth.

Syed Muhammad Ali (10)
Shaftesbury Primary School, Forest Gate

The Tick-Tocking Clock

I'm a little tick-tocking clock
That talks a lot!

I have a face
That is shaped like a case.

I need to always scour
To look for my hour.

I have three hands
And they sometimes stand.

I am a clock
That makes the sound, *tick-tock, tick-tock!*

My face beckons people
With my minutes and seconds.

I'm a good clock
That talks a lot.

Ahyan Lais (8)
Shaftesbury Primary School, Forest Gate

Books

Books, books, books, adventure books!
What are we going to find out?
Let's go outside and find out!
People think aliens are coming to Earth
Are they mad or what?

Adventures, adventures, adventures,
Adventures can be in a book!
What are we going to find out in the adventure?
Who knows?
So let's go outside and find out!
People think dinosaurs are real
Are they mad or what?

Aleeza Shah (10)
Shaftesbury Primary School, Forest Gate

Refugee

Here comes the refugee,
We may show respect,
To prove our country's worth it,
So they think we're kind.

Here comes the refugee,
We must be kind,
So they don't think we're bad.
And give them a tour of our wonderful nature.

Here comes the refugee,
Here comes the refugee,
Here comes the refugee,
Here comes the refugee.

Here comes the refugee.

Suleiman Dinki (10)
Shaftesbury Primary School, Forest Gate

The World Of Space

Why don't you go to space?
You can take yourself a case
Don't let this chance become a waste
Because you will get a taste of space.

Do aliens have a pocket?
Skip on a rocket
Don't use a socket
But don't forget to lock it.

Why do we wander in space?
The holes are like some lace
It is just as confusing as a maze,
And just like the code on a briefcase.

Hamza Delawala (10)
Shaftesbury Primary School, Forest Gate

Flying On A Cloud

Flying on a cloud is so much fun!
Zooming softly with no sound
Peacefully floating here and there
Above the ground is no sound
Having fun is what it's all about,
As high as you can fly,
Jump as high as a skyscraper
And there is your cloud
Stay as long as you like
With no fright,
Dream clouds as fluffy as pillows,
The sky as blue as an ocean
Relax on a fluffy cloud.

Aneesah Jannat Ali (8)
Shaftesbury Primary School, Forest Gate

WWIII

It's going to be WWIII
Those rumours they're telling me,
Destroy all those enemies,
We've got tanks that can destroy banks,
Soldiers lie dead, others lying in bed,
Some with bullets in their heads,
It's 2018, some are teens
Eating broccoli and beans,
All of the scientists working on artificial mist,
Once again, we shall win
It's gonna be WWIII!

Emir Rojah (10)
Shaftesbury Primary School, Forest Gate

Wonderland Fun

I'm feeling bored and jump
Into an old, dark tunnel
Seeing weird shapes up and down,
I fall to the colourful floor,
Opening a door leading to fun,
Wonderful seeing rabbits dance,
Cats talk and many more,
Eating cakes with chocolate,
Frosting having hot chocolate
With marshmallows and cream,
Royal cakes with M&M's
Everyone is happy in Wonderland.

Taneesha Anand Patel (8)
Shaftesbury Primary School, Forest Gate

The Cauldron Bubble

Double trouble, the cauldron bubbles!
The eye of a fish and the liver of a dog.

Double trouble, the cauldron bubbles!
Foot of a giraffe all decorated in a collage.

Double trouble, the cauldron bubbles!
The heart of a sheep wandering around a Jeep,
Trying to reach its feet.

Double trouble, the cauldron bubbles!
Dirty shirt, danger alert.

Zoha Rafiq (10)
Shaftesbury Primary School, Forest Gate

The Unicorn Fly

The unicorn is fluffy
The unicorn is soft
The beautiful unicorn eats rainbow food
The unicorn smells nice and beautiful
The unicorn is dreaming about rainbow food
The unicorn is lost in the park
We can't find her in the park
The unicorn is finally found
The unicorn is lovely
The unicorn is short
The unicorn is so bright.

Mariam Hussain (10)

Shaftesbury Primary School, Forest Gate

Danger Ahead

Danger is ahead
Move away, move away
Something is coming
Hide, hide, hide.

Move your feet
Into your house
Something might come
Down, down, down.

Get ready for anything
Something might come out
Bang, bang, bang!

Ruman Mahomed (11)

Shaftesbury Primary School, Forest Gate

Magical Key

I found a key,
What could it be used for?
Let's go and see
It might be for a hidden door,
Or for a treasure chest,
It could be for a cupboard,
Maybe open a door to the west,
I'm getting bored,
This can open,
My very own drawer.

Rayyan Afini (11)
Shaftesbury Primary School, Forest Gate

Jump On A Cactus

Jump on a cactus
It takes a lot of practice
Be too slow
You will have a broken toe
Sun goes down
Your roots get a frown
Be careful of the spikes
Which you do not like
The cactus is green
But sometimes mean.

Sofia Ahmed (10)
Shaftesbury Primary School, Forest Gate

Witch

The witch was scary
Someone turned off the lights
People came and ate her food
With full bellies, they slept
She wore a smile upon her big face and hat
Black gloves on her hands.

Huda Zahid (10)
Shaftesbury Primary School, Forest Gate

Mustard On Everything

Mustard on my custard
Is so delicious and tasty to me
Mustard on my spaghetti
Tastes so scrumptious to me
But some people eat ketchup and spaghetti
What a bad combination
Mustard on my jelly
Tastes like vanilla cream
What a sticky situation.

Oh what was that?
I could hear a knock at the door
I need to finish my dessert,
Oh might as well make them some
Ah, so sticky, but now I'm done
One hour later, let me now go answer the door
Oh, wait, nobody is at the door
It is only me, well that means more dessert for me.

I'm still hungry but I have mail
I'm going to open it

Why does it say too much mustard?
I never have too much mustard.

Now, I'm at the freezer
I'm going to get some vanilla ice cream
Okay, I got vanilla ice cream in the bowl
Now it's time to put on the mustard syrup
To make it even more tastier and sweeter.

My favourite time to take a mustard bath
Alright, let's jump in, *la la la la!*
Okay, I'm finished,
Time to brush my teeth with mustard
I always wonder why it tastes so weird.

I haven't been outside yet, let's go out
Oh my God, what happened?
Everything is covered in mustard and custard
Probably because of my birthday wish
Well, let's go collect all the mustard and custard.

Finally, after five trillion hours, I am done
Time to go home and sleep in my mustard bed

I'm home, time to sleep
Oh wait, I can't sleep without my mustard plush.

Jakub Czostek (9)
St James' CE Junior School, Forest Gate

Candy Catastrophe

Oh, it is amazing here on Planet Candy,
Much different to Earth
It has been my home since birth
But it changed as a huge outburst of candy
Created an explosive tornado!
Its huge head has ice coming out of its spout
It is a really bad day when it rains,
As hailstones are giant candy canes!
But, when all is well,
The gods dance on candy clouds
And we all sing out loud,
Cotton rainbows,
Prized, chocolate leprechauns,
Also with temples so large,
But with too many people, you get barged.
We love to party every night
And even bust some moves
With ancient, medieval knights!
This is a letter to our human friends,
Inviting you to join our trends!

Tayyab Ahmed Hussain (10)
St James' CE Junior School, Forest Gate

My Missing Cookies

One wonderful morning, I went to the beach
I dug out my secret cookies
Instead of a cookie, I found a map
The map led me to the sea
I looked under the sea
And I saw birds swimming as fast as fish
After, I looked up in the sky and found
Fish flying as fast as birds
Later, I looked back at the map
And the map changed
I found my hoverboard
Now it is a burger board
After, I zoomed to the middle of Earth
The map told me to look up, so I did
I found a floating island
Then I jumped up, it was amazing
The birds told the worst jokes
I ate the lollipop trees
Then, I ate the cotton candy clouds and grass
I looked up and found my cookies.

Yahyah Islam (9)
St James' CE Junior School, Forest Gate

Animals Eating The... Moon!

Whoosh! Bang! and off they go
Animals in space, watch them... woah!
Animals flying in outer space
But they're in teams because they're having a race
Cats, dogs, mice, rats
Some with clothes and some with hats
Some like Jupiter, some like Mars
Did I mention that some wore scarves!!!
But the one that was chosen the most
Was the moon and it was even given a host!
Most animals were landing on the moon
Some used forks and some used spoons
Everyone enjoyed it, they enjoyed it so much
Some even ate it for their lunch
Most missed their parents and all missed their own
So then everyone said goodbye and went home.

Maryam Ahmed (9)
St James' CE Junior School, Forest Gate

A Boy Eating Planet Mars

I saw a boy go up into space
His tummy was hungry
So he dressed red like his bed.
He knew that Mars was actually eaten
Often when people are hungry.
The boy perhaps thought
He could go up into space
And eat the planet, Mars.
His plan was to eat Mars
Before his mum came back from work.

He pulled up into space
And he tried eating Mars
He was scared, he cared about
Streaks from the stars.
He ate one bit of Mars
He said, "It's good but it
Had a little bit of goo!"

He ate and ate and became fat
So he was too heavy
For gravity to lift him

And he fell back home
His mum was so surprised.

Oniv Basu Mazumdar (8)
St James' CE Junior School, Forest Gate

Diving Giraffes

Fifty-six spotty bodies swaying on the metal
A brave one, Gretal, heading for a dive
She runs, she pants and she somersaults
Into the salty water
They don't care about anywhere
They just go slow and charge!
They shout and shriek mentally
And dive in the fresh, blue water
They duck and swim and bumped into Grim!
They came up and got out
Climbed again, this time they stand and scream
They tripped over Beam
Beam was angry and not polite
He made a fright.
Soon, they wanted to have a water fight!
Oh no... the pool keeper is coming, run!
Or you will be dead meat!
But, just five more minutes...

Samira Rahman (7)
St James' CE Junior School, Forest Gate

A Crazy Wonderland Of Animals

When you see a black cat, cross the road
That's what I am always told.
When I saw the black cat
I stood my ground
But all the cat did was purr and miaow!

They say it rains cats and dogs.
But when it rains, I see slugs and frogs.

How do they get a frog in their throat?
If they did, they would definitely croak.

Mum would say "when pigs fly,"
But if I look up high,
There are no pigs in the sky.

They say as blind as a bat,
But how do they know if they're not a bat?

Adults confuse me with what they say
But I'll use my own words to make my own way.

Layali Abdul-Aziz (7)
St James' CE Junior School, Forest Gate

The Laughing Things

First, a wacky boy who loves imaginative things
Went to a wacky forest to find weird things
He didn't find any wacky, strange animals
But he went further on and he found an alien
With pus through his nose,
Pooing through his belly button
The man said, "Ha, ha, ha, ha!"
Then he went through more things
But the alien followed him.
After that, he walked to another step
He found a strange and mysterious monster
Which pees through his earholes,
Poos through his hand.
The man felt crazy about these things
He saw disgusting things
He heard farting sounds
When they were pooing or peeing.

Ismaeel Uzzaman (9)
St James' CE Junior School, Forest Gate

Tasting The Galaxy

The stars were gummies and tasted so yellow
I went to a burger and it said, "Hello."
All the vegetables were opping out
And the patty was bigger than the bun
Oh, yes, this trip is so fun.
I went to the moon
And fried some cheesy moon rocks
Pop, pop, pop! What a strange sound.
Who knew moon rocks were so easy to make?
Travelling to the sun, I saw Saturn
You can't resist skating on Saturn's rings.
Oh, and eating some of the twisty sweets
Finally, I got to the sun
Oh, it tasted burning hot
I never knew the galaxy was so yummy
And obviously, a little bit funny.

Kayla Monica Monteiro (9)
St James' CE Junior School, Forest Gate

Bendy And The Ink Machine

When I entered the pinky inky house
I got scared and no one even cared
As I went into the main room
I found a computer that said, 'Beware'
Suddenly, it became pitch-black
And then I found a bag in a box
Filled up with dangerous soil
All put in a nice pile
"Urgh! That is gooey and slimy."
Altogether, very tight
A few minutes later,
I actually heard incredibly scary
And terrifying whispering near my ear
I was shocked and tucked down
And found a way to escape
Hopefully, I don't get jump scared
I want to say good luck to myself
Danger! I was petrified!

Kajus Milaševičius (9)
St James' CE Junior School, Forest Gate

Eating A Crunchy Moon Rock

Eating a moon rock, crunching hard
As I went to put my mouth on it
A crumbling noise, *argh!*
After a while, the noise stopped
It became quiet.

Eating my moon rock, hard and crunchy
I threw up, I felt disgusted the whole day
Never felt the same
Breathing heavily, I was miserable because...
My tooth fell out.

I slept quietly, no snoring,
No moving, nothing!
Hungry and tired, what should I do?
Eat a moon rock! My favourite,
Crunchy and crumbly, not too safe, watch out!

Later on, I'll eat all the moon rocks
And the moon will collapse.

Shakir Alin (9)
St James' CE Junior School, Forest Gate

Dragons Destroying Candy Land

I saw four little dragons
Their names were Mon, Con, Gom and Jon.
Jon was the leader
They were little but very smart.
Jon was the best liar
One day, they were playing
The loudest music I ever heard
They smashed Cookie World
Crashed Taco World
They thought they were famous.

I think they need medicine
To start all their fires
Wind comes everywhere from all that music
I run to the boxes and stop the music
I told their mum and they were never allowed
To go out of the house by themselves.

Here's a lesson kids,
Always be good to a good person.

Isabelle Tunluiaru (8)
St James' CE Junior School, Forest Gate

Adventure Bonanza

Boom! Crash! Kapow!
I woke up in a jungle
Squished up in an uncomfortable angle
Monkeys looking down at me with stink eye
While lions are having a cup of coffee, my
favourite, no lie.

Boom! Crash! Kapow!
Where am I now?
In Hogwarts watching Quidditch
On their big pitch
"Go Gryffindor!" people cheer
"Expecto patronum!" I disappear.

Boom! Crash! Kapow!
For the last time now
In outer space!
Aliens getting ready for the big race
Incy ones, bloodthirsty big ones
Furry ones, slimy ones that weigh a ton.

Aisha Saddiq (9)
St James' CE Junior School, Forest Gate

Boogie Wonderland

As we danced on top of the grey, dusty moon
All I could hear was the sound *boom, boom!*
"Can I wear these amazing shoes?"
The aliens then mooed
"This was the best party too."
More hairy aliens came,
They said, "Hey, hey, hey!"

There was a disco ball
Also, some candy bars!
Even though I was a human
The party was booming
It was nearly night
But that wasn't a fright.

Aliens were very nice
I also got to play dice with mice
That could also make rice
I ate it twice
Now I had to say bye!

Gabriella Mumenu Kinduku (9)
St James' CE Junior School, Forest Gate

Crazy Rose

Rose is a beautiful doughnut flower,
It is great, great fun
Growing among the deadly thorns,
It had never lost its beauty.

Being under the cold care of sun,
Getting the power from the winter cold sun,
It never fades but glows bright, bright, bright
It just offers to us.

Rose is red and black and beautiful
Rose, rose, rose, jump, jump, jump
The petals are black and they are like
An opening to heaven,
So joyful and sad and great.

Sunshine is so bad bright
It feeds the rose every sight
It feeds the red rose every night.

Hima Zubair (7)
St James' CE Junior School, Forest Gate

My Wonderland

W ater passes the mermaids as they swim in the sea

O n top of the hill, fly the fairies of all different colours

N an from Little Red Riding Hood lives in her house by the woods

D inosaurs roar so loud that the fairies can hear them, *roar!*

E ggs roll down the hill with Jack and Jill.

R ound circles are everywhere in Wonderland

L ittle Red Riding Hood delivers all the packages

A nabell, Thumbalina's friend is a giant

N ice dragons fly with the fairies, they are nice

D ragons soar through the sky.

Ivet Penovska (7)

St James' CE Junior School, Forest Gate

Ice Cream Poem

Ice cream in a bowl
Ice cream in a cone
Ice cream any way I want
As long as it's my own.
Ice cream can be sticky
Ice cream can be sweet
Ice cream is delicious
It's my favourite treat.
Mmm, vanilla, chocolate, strawberry
We love ice cream
Get a scoop of that,
Get a scoop of that ice cream.
Vanilla, chocolate, strawberry
Mint choc chip, butterscotch and cherry
Ice cream, ice cream, we want more
One, two, three, four, five scoops, yeah!
Ice cream, six, seven, eight,
Nine, ten scoops, yeah!
Ice cream!

Arta Siddique (7)
St James' CE Junior School, Forest Gate

Trip To The Food Solar System

On my super special twenty-second birthday
I went to the delicious food solar system.
When I arrived, it made a huge *thud!*
I looked around,
It was like a wonderland made of food.
I saw the other planets,
One looked like a huge gummy bear
That was like a piece of food
On our wonderful plant called Earth!
The gummy bear looked
Like an enormous piece of jelly.
But then, I heard a huge *crash* and *thud!*
When I turned around,
I saw a ginormous green alien
But it was a nice alien,
It was super, super hungry.

Rahell (9)
St James' CE Junior School, Forest Gate

Crazy Candy

Sunflower, sunflower, sunflower,
You're lovely and you make honey
Candy, candy, candy,
You make my mouth light up
Like popping candy
Lollipop, lollipop, lollipop,
You are hard and
You make my mouth go blue
Candyfloss, candyfloss, candyfloss,
You taste like clouds
Jelly, jelly, jelly, when I eat you,
You talk and you walk,
You have a body made out of jelly
You have a mouth, white and black eyes,
You have black hair and
You have a brown face
And a brown body
Your name is Rose and
You wear a dark pink dress.

Aniyah Opoku (8)
St James' CE Junior School, Forest Gate

Crazy Land

Wonderland, are you great?
What is that noise? It's a tornado
Wait, it's just candy, flying candy!
Yes, I was looking for it
I never ate candy in my life
My brain is always pranking me
That's why I sleep with my mum
Rumble hi-fi fo!
I smell a little toe
It's coming from the north
So a rocket ship came
I went in and instantly blasted off
It had music, it sang like this
I'm going on a ship
Which is my favourite rocket ship
Going through the years
This is a cool ship
Going through the years.

Aistis Maze (7)
St James' CE Junior School, Forest Gate

The Flying Food That Teleports You

The man sat down on his comfy couch
With a yummy bowl of cornstarch
The man stood up to get his eggs
The eggs were there
As he went to get his milk
The fridge door opened by itself
As the milk went pouring down
The man was furious
And ready to bake his cake
He put his cake in the oven
In a second, *pow!* The cake was done
He took a slice of the cake
Gobbling it up like a baby pig
Boom! Bang! Pow, pow, pow!
In the ocean with a huge splash
The cake teleported with him,
However, it flew away.

Niki Baltov (9)
St James' CE Junior School, Forest Gate

An Oreo Surfing On A Vanilla Milkshake

As I landed on a rainbow, colourful land
On my feet and took a seat
I saw the craziest thing in my life
An Oreo surfing really well!
I smelt sugary treats all around
Hearing a *splash, splash* from the vanilla shake
Then, I saw bright sprinkles from the air!
I ate so many sprinkles on my chair.
The next thing you know
I'm covered with yummy milkshake
I didn't care, I licked it all off!
Thinking to myself, *should I live here?*
A delicious adventure waiting for me every day
How I love Wonderland!

Aleena Ahmed (9)
St James' CE Junior School, Forest Gate

Unicorn Eats A Cheesecake

U nicorn, bright and fluffy!

N ever get sad and puffy

I n their world, they eat cheesecake

C ome with me, the glitter will fill your face!

O nly if you have an imagination for that land

R eady for some fun, we have awesome plans

N umber one of course, you know who they are, unicorns!

C arry your imagination with you

A nd you'll make slime with glitter glue!

K nowledge is important for us

E mpowered by magic, we ride a flying bus!

Henriqueta Djalo (9)

St James' CE Junior School, Forest Gate

Noodles Eating Kids

Noodles look at the kids dancing
Kids look at the other children happily
Suddenly, kids run over tables
Noodles attack the kids by eating the kids' hair
Some of the noodles are eating BBQ
One kid gets gobbled up
The other kids are just eating candy
Noodles hate kids
So they ate a bit of candy
While the rest jump on a candy trampoline
The noodles are angry eating kids' hair
So the noodles decide to put candy on the kids
But they are gonna eat the kids
Noodles start to sleep.

Aidan Monstaquim (8)
St James' CE Junior School, Forest Gate

Riding A Chocolate Unicorn

I ran home as fast as I could
And found a chocolate unicorn, ready to fly
I was scared at first, but found out it wasn't scary
I was really hungry
So I took a bite of the chocolate unicorn
And it regenerated itself
I kept on biting it until I was full
Suddenly, a huge thud happened
I told the chocolate unicorn
To land at my house
I ran inside my room
Because I thought it was a giant
From that day on, when I was sad
I would take a ride with the chocolate unicorn.

Matyas Sarosi (9)
St James' CE Junior School, Forest Gate

Marvellous Skeleton

The most marvellous skeleton
Was invited to a party
He wanted to be
The most beautiful skeleton in the party
Then he had a perfect idea!
He wanted to paint his nails rainbow
In a flash, he got ready and go!
Then his best friend called Mamade jumped for joy
Skeleton was so annoyed with his friend
That he danced instead
When the judges were going to choose
Skeleton was exhausted
Then the answer was Skeleton
He won because of his nails
He got a crown and won!

Maria Galarza (9)
St James' CE Junior School, Forest Gate

Somersaulting Giraffes

The giraffes are splashing and somersaulting
In the dark, deep water
The silly giraffes are diving into the salty water
The spotty, furry giraffes are running
And pushing other giraffes
In the scary, deep water.
The lovely, warm water is cooling
The giraffes down to make them energised.
A silly giraffe is hanging from the light
And making other giraffes somersault and dive.
The giraffes are somersaulting
From the really high diving board
Into a really deep pool.

Iqlas Abukar (7)
St James' CE Junior School, Forest Gate

Giraffes Diving

Find a brown, speckled giraffe
Going to a pool centre
Galloping to the pool, diving into the pool
A giraffe hanging on the rooftop
What happens next? He is ready to dive
Then a pale, brown, speckled giraffe
Diving like a cow
He splashes loud
The next giraffe gets on the top
And does a backflip, the pool keeper wakes up
Oh no! They're going to be seen
The giraffes shower and run out of the pool centre
They go back home to sleep
Yay, they escaped!

Raphael Kimuli (7)
St James' CE Junior School, Forest Gate

Dreamland

I'm stuck here in Dreamland
With nothing to do,
I'm ever so bored, but is that true?

I can jump up high, and fly
As my cat walks by
With three tails!
Oh, she looks kinds of pale!

As I jump up high,
Out of my socks,
I can see in the bush,
A naughty fox
With chocolate round its mush!

As I wake up from my dream,
I say bye to weird things
And hello to normal, boring things
Though I'm still snoring.

Sophie Chambers (9)
St James' CE Junior School, Forest Gate

Giraffes Diving Into Water

Funny, tall giraffes laughing a lot
Like a funny clown
Diving into the water dangerously
But the rules are: no chatting,
No shouting, no screaming
The rules are here to save your life!
When you dive in the water,
You might imagine there are sharks around!
Run for your lives, go to bed
And make sure you don't go to the water again
Giant giraffes gobbling some apples like a parrot
When you got to sleep again,
Creep out to play outside.

Liyana Haque (7)
St James' CE Junior School, Forest Gate

Junk Food Becomes Healthy Food

Today, when I woke up, I found out
The breakfast was chocolate
Not an apricot
I was shocked to see such a thing
And thought to myself, *what's happening?*
Then my mum came and said with a smile,
"Junk has become healthy food,
Healthy has become junk food!"
So I went to Google
And ordered some noodles
I had a lot of fun
By eating a chocolate bun
For dessert, I had an ice cream
And my alarm rang, it was a dream.

Siyona Paliwal (9)
St James' CE Junior School, Forest Gate

Giraffes Eating Bubblegum That Makes You Fly In To A Pool

Giraffes eating bubblegum, just one bite or two
When they take some of it, they will go twit twoo
Twit twoo into the sky,
But I don't know if they will die
In the beautiful sky, but if they die
And see a raft in the sky
They will dream of cotton candy
All day and all night
But at least I don't like bubblegum
So I won't go pop or make slop go everywhere
So whatever I do, I won't die, will you?

Dion Byne (7)
St James' CE Junior School, Forest Gate

The Giraffe Team

The giraffes clamber around
Finding a pool for their award
The pool keeper's asleep
And the giraffes dive in one at a time
They do backflips and dive
And quietly go back in line
They dive back in and out
They use their legs to dive in and swim out
To get to the end of the line
They take a bow and back of the line
Before the pool keeper wakes
They make a dash for it, goodbye.

Ihsaan Uzzaman (8)
St James' CE Junior School, Forest Gate

Who Is Knocking On The Door?

Who is knocking on the door?
An alien that can speak English?
A postman with bunny ears?
Who is knocking on the magical door?
Miss Jones? Miss Bee?
I am madly confused, I wonder who it is
I am not sure who it is, that is crazy
And knocking on the door
Why can't I ever know?
Ah, it is Dad! Yay!
It is time to go to the beach
Time to go and pack
Bye-bye.

Rachael Oluwagbemisola Akinnifesi (7)
St James' CE Junior School, Forest Gate

Abducted By Aliens!

Once there was a dog that lived on a bog,
That got abducted by aliens!

They dropped him to the bog,
He had the power to fly
He flew then he found some sausages
He flew all the way.

Then he shouted, "No way!"
The sausages could talk
And they were smart.

They were best friends forever
They went on adventures together.

Aritz Ayomikun Akinrele (8)
St James' CE Junior School, Forest Gate

Guessing Game

The weird and wonderful guessing game

Who is it?
A tall and smart-looking woman
Smartly dressed with dashing glasses.

Boss of all students
As she is working
Whilst we are learning.

Who is it?
Someone as happy as a celebrity
All she drinks is nice, warm tea
Live to learn, learn to live.

Who can it be? Who is it?

Ethan Bennet (7)
St James' CE Junior School, Forest Gate

Diving Giraffes

Thirty speckled giraffes
Diving into the swimming pool
Without the pool keeper's permission.
The rules are: no running, screaming
And no getting out of the pool
Without the pool keeper's permission
But whatever the rules are,
They would not listen to the rules.
The pool keeper must keep the giraffes safe
The pool keeper's awake, run!

Amin Mosthafa (7)
St James' CE Junior School, Forest Gate

The Lion Without A Name

Tourists say, "Have you heard
Of the lion without a mane?"
He's got big, bad, yellow teeth.
His claws are as sharp as a needle
That hasn't been cut
He's got a perfect smell but a lost mane
Have you heard the sound
Of crying and roaring
In your evening dreams
And remember the tale
Of the lion without a mane."

Zak Abdo (7)
St James' CE Junior School, Forest Gate

Underground Swimming

D irt is going in my ear holes
I n this secret lair, there are wild moles
R avenously swimming, I see a green thing
T urtles are the thing, they go like *ping!*

L azily, I stopped
A nxiously, my brain popped
I saw a load of gold
R andomly, my face went cold.

Ruwaydah Alin (9)
St James' CE Junior School, Forest Gate

Giraffes Diving

Seven skinny-legged giraffes
Crazily running to the pool
So they can be cool as a coconut
So very talented and very crazy
They jump like a bouncing ball
They are really tall and really silly
And really skinny
Giraffes don't care about their safety
They just want to have some fun
In the sun with everyone.

Diyana Ahmed (7)
St James' CE Junior School, Forest Gate

Winter Wonderland

Dear Winter Wonderland,
I like snow, but I want it to be warm
At the same time
I like to make snowmen
With my big sister, Lily
And my big brother, Stanley
We have snowball fights
And we go inside for hot food
We brush our teeth
And we have a hot shower
We watch TV and go to sleep.

Renee Anselm (7)
St James' CE Junior School, Forest Gate

P.O.E.T.

Who took a P from pluck?
Now they have all my luck.

Who shot the O from a shout?
I'm stuck in this place and the door's shut.

Who stole the E from this poet?
I just found an empty pot.

Who robbed the T from a track?
My hat is on a rack.

P.O.E.T.

Ibrahim Njie (9)
St James' CE Junior School, Forest Gate

Diving Giraffes

The giraffes are climbing
The pool keeper's asleep
The two have fun with a rainbow leap
No splashing, no jumping,
Shhh! Be quiet
The pool keeper's asleep
One, two, three... *splash!*
Come, the pool keeper's awake
Let's just go to the lake.

Khadeeja Hassan Mallu (7)
St James' CE Junior School, Forest Gate

A Princess Who Can Eat So Much Candy

A princess is smart and beautiful,
But this princess is not smart or beautiful
This princess is cool, a goody
One night, she went downstairs
And ate all the candy
And then she went to sleep
Who was she?
Is she a cloud? What is her name?
Her name is Blossom.

Alisa Emini (7)
St James' CE Junior School, Forest Gate

Miss Daniel

I am going to sleep, I see a giant giraffe
And a unicorn with a wizard
A big cat, but the giraffes are exciting
The giraffes are tall
The pool caretaker is crossing
Getting sweet candy in Candy Land
I love my dream, I wake up
I saw a giraffe in my pool.

Shakira Sulekhan (7)
St James' CE Junior School, Forest Gate

Giraffes Diving Into The Pool

The giraffes are tall
The pool caretaker is asleep
The giraffes have long legs
The pool caretaker is unaware
The water is like soft candyfloss
The cheeky giraffes dive into the deep pool
The giraffes are funny
As funny as a clumsy monster.

Remai Peart (7)
St James' CE Junior School, Forest Gate

Swimming Unicorn

Forty giraffes diving in the pure blue pool
No running, no pushing, no talking
The big, fat pool keepers and two security guards
Are asleep, nearly time, we have to be quiet
The guards are awake, hurry and go!
The bell rang, so go to the exit door.

Ayaan Amer (7)
St James' CE Junior School, Forest Gate

Moon Life

Moon life is great
I used flying pigs with wings
What magical things.
Moon life is great
I built a house with a mouse
The rocks were made of cheese
For lunch, I made peace.
Moon life is great
I found aliens that were my mates.

Anayet Noor (9)
St James' CE Junior School, Forest Gate

Having A Bath On The Moon

I have a bath on the moon
I wonder if I am weird
Am I weird? Who knows?
I might need to go
Wait no, so am I weird?
My bubbles in my bath
Are bubbling like a kettle
But I better settle
Soon I am going to have a moon bath.

Marouan Ouldmakhloufi (9)
St James' CE Junior School, Forest Gate

Giraffes Diving

First, some giraffes came along
Then they walked and walked for a second
Then one of them ran and swung on a pole
Then the giraffe splashed happily in the cold water
Then the others did the same
And they were so noisy.

Farhan Omar Kazi (7)
St James' CE Junior School, Forest Gate

Giraffes Splashing Splash

Giraffe dives look like
They're in the dark blue sky
Creeping slowly
When they see the pool man
He looks funny
They jump high
Then do you hear a noise?
No splashing!
I do. *Quack, quack!*

Mariam Zakaria (7)
St James' CE Junior School, Forest Gate

Giraffes Jumping Into The Swimming Pool

Quick, the tall team, flipping, dripping
Catches to show their tricks
Running like crazy
Throwing their bodies into the pool
They're scared like cats
Because they don't want to wake the pool keeper.

Abubakar Hussain (7)

St James' CE Junior School, Forest Gate

Giraffes Diving Underwater

The ten speckled giraffes walking on the board
One falls down on the statue of the Lord
Don't dive and drown all the way down
Don't dive to die, remember to save lives
The lake is like a snake.

Amirah Begum (7)
St James' CE Junior School, Forest Gate

Under The Sea

A mermaid walking a bag
And a monkey under the sea
Under the sea and under the sea school
I see a fish swimming away from the shark
Crabs dancing with a dolphin
Mermaid walking a dog to school

Destiny Boima (8)
St James' CE Junior School, Forest Gate

Unicorns Are The Best

Unicorns are beautiful and white
Unicorns are magical and gorgeous
Unicorns are powerful and strong
It's spiralling horn does magic
They have a rainbow mane
And that makes me happy.

Selena Saimyer (7)
St James' CE Junior School, Forest Gate

Giraffes Breaking The Rules

Twenty-four speckled stick feet
Walking on the pool
No pushing, no running, no screaming, no dives
Whatever the rules, they are meant to save lives
Tiptoeing to the pool without any noise.

Aleena Hoque (7)
St James' CE Junior School, Forest Gate

Giraffes Diving In The Water

Giraffe, giraffe, what are you doing?
Splish, splash, don't wake him up
Then don't run away
He'll wake up and find you gone away
But be happy.

Maryam Khatun (7)
St James' CE Junior School, Forest Gate

Mrs Daniel

The giraffes are tall
The pool's caretaker is asleep
The giraffes have long legs and long necks
The pool caretaker is cross
The water is cold.

Perla Alegra Petkeviciute (7)
St James' CE Junior School, Forest Gate

YOUNG WRITERS INFORMATION

We hope you have enjoyed reading this book – and that you will continue to in the coming years.

If you're a young writer who enjoys reading and creative writing, or the parent of an enthusiastic poet or story writer, do visit our website **www.youngwriters.co.uk**. Here you will find free competitions, workshops and games, as well as recommended reads, a poetry glossary and our blog. There's lots to keep budding writers motivated to write!

If you would like to order further copies of this book, or any of our other titles, then please give us a call or visit **www.youngwriters.co.uk**.

Young Writers
Remus House
Coltsfoot Drive
Peterborough
PE2 9BF
(01733) 890066
info@youngwriters.co.uk

Join in the conversation!
Tips, news, giveaways and much more!

 YoungWritersUK    @YoungWritersCW